GOLDFISH

edited by Paul R. Paradise

D1248098

(1) A nearly perfect pair of metallic fantails. (2) This is what the original goldfish, *Carassius auratus,* looked like. (3) The golden orfe, *Leuciscus idus,* is a small coldwater fish that does well in a goldfish pond. (4) Another *Carassius* species closely related to the goldfish.

CONTENTS:
History and Description, 8; Setting Up, 24; Aquarium Maintenance, 34; The Garden Pond, 44; Breeding Goldfish, 54; Goldfish Varieties, 62; Foods and Feeding, 68; Diseases, Injuries and Parasites, 80.

Back Cover: Courtesy Wardley Products Co.
Front Endpapers: Photo by Dr. Herbert R. Axelrod.

ISBN 0-87666-511-3
KW-014

Distributed in the UNITED STATES by T.F.H. Publications, Inc., 211 West Sylvania Avenue, Neptune City, NJ 07753; in CANADA by H & L Pet Supplies Inc., 27 Kingston Crescent, Kitchener, Ontario N2B 2T6; Rolf C. Hagen Ltd., 3225 Sartelon Street, Montreal 382 Quebec; in ENGLAND by T.F.H. (Great Britain) Ltd., 11 Ormside Way, Holmethorpe Industrial Estate, Redhill, Surrey RH1 2PX; in AUSTRALIA AND THE SOUTH PACIFIC by T.F.H. (Australia) Pty. Ltd., Box 149, Brookvale 2100 N.S.W., Australia; in NEW ZEALAND by Ross Haines & Son, Ltd., 18 Monmouth Street, Grey Lynn, Auckland 2 New Zealand; in SINGAPORE AND MALAYSIA by MPH Distributors Pte., 71-77 Stamford Road, Singapore 0617; in the PHILIPPINES by Bio-Research, 5 Lippay Street, San Lorenzo Village, Makati, Rizal; in SOUTH AFRICA by Multipet Pty. Ltd., 30 Turners Avenue, Durban 4001. Published by T.F.H. Publications Inc., Ltd., the British Crown Colony of Hong Kong. THIS IS THE 1983 EDITION.

1

2

3

(1) A pair of veiltails. Note the smooth egg shape of the body. (2) This is a Bristol shubunkin. It has nacreous scales toward the rear of the body. (3) The Cambridge blue comet is one of the hardiest goldfish types and does especially well in an outdoor pool.

(1) This is a two-year-old adult veiltail with a nearly perfect body shape. Note the smooth unbroken curve of the back. Photo by Laurence E. Perkins. (2) Good veiltails such as these show a nearly perfect egg shape to the head and abdomen. Photo by Klaus Paysan.

History

and

Description

Goldfish have been with us for more than 300 years. The typical goldfish as we know it today does not occur in the wild but was bred by the Chinese from natural mutations of the wild Crucian carp, a popular food fish. While goldfish were mentioned in Chinese poetry as early as 800 AD, it is believed that they did not arrive in Europe until about 1600—they were frequently mentioned by learned European authors of that era. The original wild variety of goldfish still exists in rivers and sluggish streams of its native China, where its somber olive color blends in with murky waters, providing the fish with excellent camouflage. Even today, the young of most domesticated goldfish varieties start life with the same somber coloring, only at-

1   2

(1) Moors are usually seen as black fish. This young black moor has the telescope-eye feature and is a veiltail variety. This specimen lacks metallic reflections in the scales—a desirable quality in this strain. (2) This is the lionhead. It features a soft, fleshy head growth (hood) and lacks a dorsal fin. It is not a very able swimmer, probably because of its lack of a dorsal fin, so its competition should be minimized by not keeping it with other strains. (3) This is the celestial goldfish. It, too, lacks a dorsal fin, and its odd eye position limits its vision to that which is above it. Photos by H. Hansen, Aquarium Berlin.

taining the peak of their characteristic golden hue when they are about one year old.

Because of their beautiful coloring and often extreme hardiness, goldfish have become one of the most popular pets in the world. So popular are they, that they are given away at carnivals and circuses in games of chance! Until recently, a spherical or drum-shaped bowl containing a couple of miserable-looking goldfish was a common feature in many homes. Unknown to their well-intentioned keepers, however, the very shape of the bowl provided an insufficient surface area for the absorption of oxygen and the dissipation of carbon dioxide, giving them a very lethargic appearance. Fortunately, this "fishbowl" concept is almost a thing of the past in western countries, and goldfish are now being displayed in rectangular tanks or, even more appropriately, in garden ponds.

The goldfish, *Carassius auratus,* belongs to the carp family, which is known as Cyprinidae. Most carp possess barbels on their lips, but in the case of the Crucian carp from which most goldfish are derived the barbels are absent, making the differentiation between the goldfish and Crucian carp often very difficult. The easiest method of distinguishing them from one another is to look at the shape of the dorsal fin—that of the goldfish is normally straight or slightly concave, while that of the Crucian carp is usually convex.

Over the centuries breeders have produced many weird and bizarre goldfish varieties, but it was the Japanese who, by selective breeding, produced a great many of the varieties known to us today.

External Features

Many people, when thinking of a pet fish, envision a common goldfish. The common goldfish possesses all of the typical fish characteristics: streamlined and scale-covered body, gill covers, large lidless eyes, large mouth and, of course, fins.

The fins of a fish have three main functions: stabilization, braking and, to some extent, propulsion. It is the caudal fin that seems to show the greatest variation between goldfish strains, often appearing as a single fin, a paired fin or any intermediate variation with pointed, squared, forked, rounded, short or long ends.

To obtain the necessary oxygen, fish draw water through the mouth, over the delicate gill filaments and finally pass it out through the opercula or gill covers. This process removes precious oxygen from the water via fine capillaries in the gill filaments and passes it into the fish's bloodstream, just as oxygen is removed via lung capillaries in higher vertebrates. Simultaneously, carbon dioxide is expelled from the bloodstream and discharged into the water passing over the gills, thus the fish's respiratory wastes are removed from its body just as similar wastes are removed from our body via our lungs. When the water is polluted or deficient in oxygen as it often is in a typical "goldfish bowl," the goldfish congregate at the surface where the oxygen is being dissolved into the water. When goldfish hang from the surface with their gills making popping noises, they are actually gasping for oxygen in the air to avoid suffocation. This behavior indicates, of course, that the fish need immediate attention.

Unlike most higher animals, in which the nostrils open internally into the respiratory system, the nostrils of fishes are merely dead-end pits that house scent buds. The scent buds are innervated and connect via the nervous system directly to the brain.

Fish possess no external ears, although they do have an internal "ear" or labyrinth. The labyrinth serves the fish mostly as an organ of balance rather than hearing. To detect noises or vibrations in the water most fishes have a lateral line. This consists of a row of pores that runs

(1) An adult lionhead with a well-developed hood. (2) Hood development has just begun in these 18-month-old female lionheads and will not be complete until the fish are three to four years old. (3) Head-up or head-down, visual acuity is not one of the strengths of the celestial goldfish. (4) These are good specimens of the common goldfish. (5) The fringe along the fin edges in these veiltails is not a desirable trait. Photos by Laurence E. Perkins.

1

2

3

4

5

(1) The intermingling of black, orange, red and white is quite variable on veiltail goldfish. (2) The fin edges on this veiltail are a bit too ragged. (3) The caudal fin is disproportionately short on this veiltail. (4) Note the nice smooth profile to the fins and body of this veiltail. (5) *Carassius carassius* has a convex margin to its dorsal fin rather than concave as in the goldfish. Photo by J. Elias. Photos 1, 2, 3, and 4 by Laurence E. Perkins.

4

5

17

(1) A two-year-old hammer-scale. This is one of several scale mutants. Photo by Laurence E. Perkins. (2) This is a Russian-bred oranda. It has a hood like the lionhead, but it also has a dorsal fin. Photo by Kochetov. (3) This young comet will probably lose most of its black color as it matures. Photo courtesy of Wardley Products Co. (4) Most goldfish are fairly docile and can be kept together in a mixture of sizes and breeds.

1

2

3

4

horizontally along the sides of the fish. The pores contain nerve cells or neuromasts and are interconnected by a canal that runs under the skin. The neuromasts in each pore are also interconnected and run directly to the brain via the same cranial nerve that connects to the ears in higher animals.

The eyes of goldfish are fairly large, lidless and are somewhat movable. Goldfish are generally believed to be nearsighted, but their eyesight seems to be adequate for their needs. Highly developed goldfish strains having telescope and bubble eyes have a more restricted field of vision than goldfish having normal eyes do, but when they are well cared for in an aquarium they seem to have no difficulty finding their way around.

The body of the goldfish is covered with overlapping scales which are hard plates set beneath a thin layer of epidermal tissue. The scales offer the fish protection against injury and infection. There are also numerous mucous glands in the skin that produce the characteristic slimy surface on the fish. This slime coating also protects the fish against injury and disease and, in addition, reduces friction between the fish and its watery environment, making it easier for the fish to swim.

The size of the scales varies with the size and age of the fish. Good scale shape and definition are important in creating the correct body outline. All goldfish have scales, but some strains are erroneously known as "scaleless." On these fish the scales are less conspicuous because they lack the layer of pigment sometimes known as guanine that normally renders them opaque and gives them their metallic iridescence. The amount of this pigment apparent in a fish is at least partly governed by inheritance but is also governed by environmental factors such as the fish's food. According to the Goldfish Society of Great Britain, the goldfish that do not have much of this reflective pigment in their scales are termed "matt" fish, while fish having a good supply of guanine under all of their scales are termed "metallic." Goldfish with a combination of metallic and matt scales are called "nacreous." Genetically speaking, neither metallic nor matt scales are completely dominant. Nacreous appears to be an intermediate state of scale coloration that is produced by crossing a metallic fish to a matt fish. Goldfish whose scales are entirely of the matt type are seldom seen commercially because they do not show the intense coloration of the metallic fish, and they do not seem to be as hardy either.

Each variety of goldfish has a specific number of scales that remains constant, barring accidental loss. As the fish grows, each scale grows at its periphery. During the winter when the water is cooler, the goldfish's growth slows down or stops altogether, depending upon how cool it is kept. When the pond water warms up again in the spring and the fish once more begins to feed heavily, rapid growth starts again. This slowing down and reacceleration of the growth process causes rings to form on the scales, and the number of rings on each scale indicates the age of the fish—one ring representing one year's growth.

At 60 days of age, most goldfish that hatch having the protective Crucian coloration usually begin to lose their color. The scales blacken and then begin to fade, starting at the belly area and progressing upward toward the back. When these fish have completed this phase they are usually yellow in color, but with the passage of time their color intensifies, once more giving them a darker appearance. Not all goldfish strains undergo this decoloration. Some may never decolor while others may not do so until they are several years old. Matt fish never pass through this color change because they hatch light in color (often white) and gradually darken as their colors intensify. The ultimate color of a goldfish is strongly influenced by its diet and the chemical composition of the water in which it is reared as well as its genetic endowments.

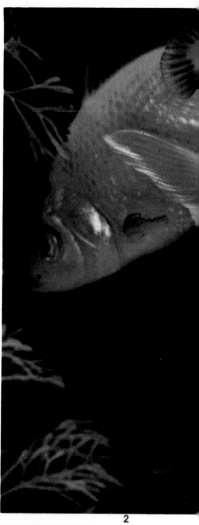

1

2

3

(1) Nacreous calico fan-tails. (2) This gleaming metallic color has been bred into most goldfish strains. (3) The comet has an ordinary body shape, but the lobes of the tail fin are elongated. (4) The common goldfish has no exaggerated finnage.

4

(1) Gravel or sand should be washed thoroughly before it is put into the pond or aquarium. Here cold water is being run through the sand, and the washing will be complete when the water running out of the bucket runs clear. (2) Sand, gravel and rocks can be tastefully combined to provide an interesting aquascape. Photo by H.F. Cate.

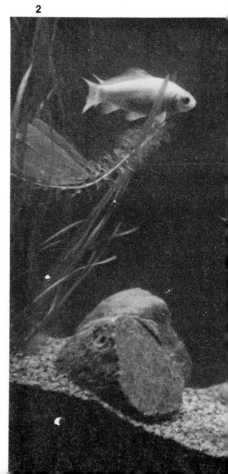

Setting Up

Your goldfish aquarium should be purchased, set up and aged before you buy the fish. In order to purchase the right aquarium, you should have some idea of the kind and number of goldfish you want to buy, but we'll discuss buying the goldfish a little later. First, let's look at the procedure for selecting the right equipment and setting it up.

The Aquarium

If you intend to become a serious goldfish keeper, you should consider purchasing a standard rectangular aquarium rather than the traditional "goldfish bowl." To properly keep a one-inch goldfish you should have at least a one-gallon aquarium with a water surface area of about 70 to 90

(1) A young oranda going through its color changing phases. The black head cap, black ring around the eyes and the black snout look almost as if they were intentionally bred into this fish. It is unfortunate that this interesting color pattern will change as the fish matures. Photo by Dr. Herbert R. Axelrod. (2) The eye sacs are well formed on this celestial bubble-eye goldfish. Photo by R. Zukal. (3) Typical color varieties in the common goldfish.

3

square inches. This automatically excludes most bowls. While a one-gallon bowl may hold the right amount of water for a small goldfish, most bowls are round and narrower at the top than they are in the middle. If a one-gallon bowl is filled with water, the water surface near the top is much less than it is at the middle of the bowl. But if you fill the bowl only to the middle it will not have enough water in it for the goldfish to be comfortable for a very long period of time.

A rectangular aquarium has the same surface area at the center as it does at the top. Maximum air-water interface is important because most of the oxygen in the water is absorbed at the surface. By restricting this surface, as you would in a bowl, there will not be enough oxygen in the water for the fish to breathe properly. This large surface is also important to the goldfish because it allows a greater amount of carbon dioxide to be dispelled from the water than a small surface area would allow. In addition to lack of oxygen, excess carbon dioxide will cause the fish to suffocate.

While a one-inch goldfish can be kept in a one-gallon aquarium, that does not necessarily mean that a 10-inch goldfish can be kept in a 10-gallon aquarium. The amount of oxygen a fish consumes is determined by the fish's mass or weight, not by its length. A 10-inch goldfish weighs much more than 10 times the weight of a one-inch goldfish, because in addition to being much longer, it is also much larger in girth. If your goldfish are well cared for and well fed, they are going to grow quickly. With a few months of good care a one-inch goldfish can grow to a length of several inches, so a 10-gallon aquarium will not comfortably house 10 one-inch goldfish either. A 10-gallon aquarium is 20 inches long and 10 inches wide, so it has a surface area of about 200 square inches. This means that it can comfortably house three or four small goldfish and will allow plenty of room for them to swim and grow. A five-gallon aquarium can comfortably hold a pair of small goldfish, and a 20-gallon tank (the 30-inch long style) can comfortably house six to eight fish. These aquariums can be more crowded than this, but that means more cleaning, more water changing and stronger filtration will be required.

The Bottom

A one- to two-inch layer of sand or gravel should be placed on the bottom of the aquarium. The gravel will anchor the aquarium plants and will provide a more natural looking environment for your goldfish. The sand or gravel should be fairly fine in texture (a 1/8th-inch particle size is just about right). Coarser gravel will allow uneaten food particles to become trapped in the gravel bed where they will decay, fouling the water and causing it to become cloudy with harmful, smelly bacteria.

The gravel should be washed before placing it in the tank. This is easily accomplished by putting it in a clean pan (making sure there is no soap or detergent residue in the pan) and running a strong flow of tapwater through the gravel, occasionally stirring it, until the water runs off clean and clear.

Colored gravels can be used in the goldfish aquarium. Just make sure that the gravel purchased is color-fast; that is, make sure it is not the type that will lose its dye in the water. While tinted water usually will not harm the fishes, it certainly does not make them look very attractive! Most colored gravels manufactured specifically for aquarium use are color-fast. The use of a dark gravel such as black, dark green or dark blue gives the goldfish their best appearance. Lighter gravels will give the fish a washed out look.

Plants in the Aquarium

While goldfish can be maintained quite successfully without the presence of live plants in the aquarium (many peo-

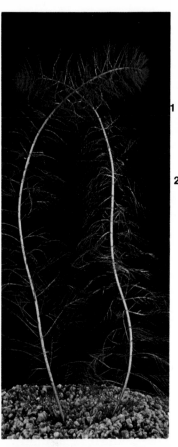

(1) *Myriophyllum scabratum* grows well in ponds and well-lit aquaria. Photo by R. Zukal. (2) Several parrot's feather or *Myriophyllum* species are available, and most of them grow profusely in garden ponds. Photo by Charles O. Masters. (3) *Vallisneria americana* reproduces quickly by sending out root runners. Photo by T. J. Horeman. (4) *Bacopa monniera* makes a good background plant if given plenty of light. Photo by R. Zukal. (5) Water lilies are a favorite for outdoor goldfish ponds. Photo by Dr. Herbert R. Axelrod. (6) Aquatic irises make fine border plants for garden ponds. Photo by Charles O. Masters. (7) Water lettuce provides good shading to prevent ponds from overheating. Photo by Dr. Herbert R. Axelrod.

4

5

6

7

ple prefer plastic plants since they require no maintenance and look very real), they are easier to keep healthy if live plants are present. The value of aquarium plants, as providers of oxygen, is limited. As mentioned earlier, most oxygen is taken into the water at the surface from the atmosphere.

Be sure the plants you buy are green and healthy. Expensive plants for goldfish aquariums are not necessary, because most goldfish will nibble on them at times, and you wouldn't want to have an expensive plant destroyed. The best plants to begin with are *Elodea* or anacharis as it is often called and *Cabomba*. Both are inexpensive, grow rapidly just floating in the water and don't require special care other than sufficient lighting either from a sunlit window or from an aquarium light fixture. Once the aquarium is well established and the fish and plants are flourishing (usually this happens after a few months of good care), you can put some strongly rooted plants in the tank such as *Vallisneria, Sagittaria, Ludwigia* or Amazon swordplants.

The Water

Goldfish, even very fancy strains, are coldwater fish, so they don't require heated aquarium water. Room-temperature water suits them well. But, like any other animal, they are liable to become ill if they are exposed to sudden drastic temperature changes, especially if the temperature is suddenly dropped. When their water needs to be changed, make sure the fresh water is at the same temperature as that which they are already in. The best way to do this is to keep a plastic or glass jug of water stored in the same general area the aquarium is kept in so that its temperature will be about the same.

In addition to equalizing the temperature, storing the water allows enough time for the chlorine in it to dissipate into the air. The amount of chlorine in most tapwater will kill goldfish, so it must somehow be removed from the water before the water can be used. Storing the water for at least 24 hours allows that to happen naturally. It's a good idea to keep a bottle of chemical chlorine remover handy in case your goldfish need a complete water change quickly when there is no aged water available.

As a part of routine maintenance, one-fourth to one-third of the aquarium water should be changed weekly. For a small partial change like this, fresh tapwater can be used without worrying about the chlorine in it harming your goldfish. The fresh water will be greatly diluted by the remaining old water in your aquarium so the chlorine will not be concentrated enough to harm the fish. But the temperature must still be equalized before adding the new water to the aquarium. This can be simply done by using the right mixture of hot and cold tapwater.

Buying the Goldfish

Later on in this book, specifics of many goldfish varieties will be discussed, but there are certain conditions to look for when buying any variety. It's important to make sure the goldfish you buy is healthy. While the fish is still in the dealer's tank look at the fins to be sure they are not chewed up or torn. While torn fins heal quickly when the fish is kept in a clean healthy aquarium, buying an already injured fish is not a good idea. Moving the fish from the dealer's tank to your tank could cause other problems to occur in an already injured fish. Look closely at the scales of the fish to make certain that none are missing. There should not be any blood spots on the body or fins. The mouth should not have any whitish areas on it or around it. The fish should be pert and active in the dealer's tank. If the fish is swimming sluggishly or not moving at all and the fins are not open, the fish may not be healthy and should not be purchased.

(1) Weekly siphoning from the bottom of the tank and replacing about one-fourth to one-third of the water with fresh tapwater will result in a healthy flourishing aquarium (2). Photos by G. Stephen Dow.

Aquarium Maintenance

Now that the tank has been set up, planted and the fish have been introduced, regular maintenance should be your primary goal. Obviously, when considerable time has been devoted to making the aquarium as attractive and as natural-looking as possible, it is important that it be well maintained. A balanced tank should not require a great deal of upkeep, perhaps only a few minutes a week. It is best to set aside a certain time each week for this purpose, and you should look forward to it with pleasure rather than looking at maintenance as a chore. A word of warning is necessary at this point. It is possible to overmaintain an aquarium. Fish and plants will suffer if they are disturbed too often.

After a few weeks the aquarium will become "mature."

This means that colonies of beneficial bacteria have become established in the tank and are effectively converting fish wastes into materials that are harmless to the fish but useful to the plants.

At this time algae will begin to appear in the tank. Algae are a low form of plant life, the spores of which can travel freely in both water and air. Eventually algal spores will find their way into almost any aquarium. There are many algal species that can become established in the aquarium—some are bright green and others are brown or reddish brown. Most algal species are beneficial to the aquarium in limited quantities. They provide some fresh food for the fish, to a limited degree they help oxygenate the water and they absorb some of the byproducts of fish wastes as their food. The main problem with algae is that they grow all over the inner glass surfaces of the aquarium and make it difficult to see the fish. For a clear view of the fish, algae should be removed from the front glass and perhaps from the sides, too. This can be done with an inexpensive algae scraper purchased from a pet shop, or you can use a single-edge razor blade as long as you are careful not to scratch the glass. Because of its benefit to the aquarium and the fishes, it's a good idea to leave some of the algae in the tank, for instance on the back glass and on any rocks you have in the tank. In addition to the benefits mentioned above, a small amount of algae also helps give the tank a more natural appearance.

Live plants should be inspected often, and any dead or dying leaves or shoots should be removed. They can be easily removed by pinching them off between the thumb and forefinger. From time to time it may be necessary to prune those plants that have grown too large. Cuttings from plants such as *Cabomba*, anacharis or water sprite can be retained for planting in another tank or for starting new clumps of plants in the original tank. Sometimes hair-like algae spread throughout the tank, covering rocks and plants with long green threads. This algae can be removed from the plants by gently passing your fingers through the foliage then scooping out the floating threads with a net.

A certain amount of sediment or mulm will build up on the surface of the gravel bed. This sediment consists of dead pieces of plants, decomposed remains of uneaten food particles and fish droppings. Some of this material will work its way into the gravel bed and provide nourishment for rooted plants. The remainder, although relatively harmless to the fish, looks rather unpleasant and should be periodically removed. This can be done by siphoning it off the bottom. To siphon the tank you will need a three- or four-foot-long piece of rubber or plastic hose with an inside diameter of about one-fourth to three-eighths of an inch and a bucket. First fill the hose with water by totally submersing it in the tank and allowing all of the air in it to bubble out. Then, placing your thumbs over both ends of the hose to keep the water in it, lift one end out of the tank, over the edge and down toward the bucket. Releasing your thumbs from both ends of the hose simultaneously will start the siphon, thus emptying the water into the bucket. With one hand aim the hose toward the bucket, and with the other hand guide the submersed end of the hose over the bottom, far enough away from the gravel so that no gravel is sucked into the hose, but close enough to remove the mulm. This is the ideal time to make your regular water change, so allow one-fourth to one-third of the water to empty into the bucket. Then replace the water with temperature-adjusted aged water or fresh tapwater as discussed in the last chapter.

Sometimes a layer of dust or scum will form on the surface of the water. This should be removed, as it will retard the exchange of gases between the water and the atmosphere. Lay a single sheet of clean newspaper on the surface of the water until it begins to soak—this happens almost immediately. Then remove the paper by more or

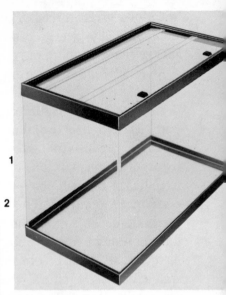

1

2

3

4

6

(1) A tight-fitting aquarium cover is essential for good aquarium management. (2) Inside box filters are available in several different sizes and styles. (3) Aquarium heaters can help control the warming of a cold winter aquarium for goldfish breeding but are not necessary for goldfish during most of the year. (4) Special siphon hoses are available to clean surface gravel. (5) Pet shops carry a wide assortment of special purpose foods that are beneficial to tropical fish and goldfish. (6) Undergravel filters are available to fit nearly any size aquarium.

5

1

2

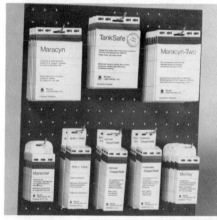

4

3

(1) Filter material is available in precut pads of several different sizes or in sheets which can be cut to any size. (2) No goldfish aquarium should be without a reliable airpump. There are sizes available to fit the needs of any aquarist. (3) and (4) Most pet shops carry an assortment of medications to cure almost any common goldfish disease.

less sliding it off the surface of the water. Most of the scum will be removed with the paper. It may be necessary to repeat this a few times in order to remove all of the scum—a clean sheet of dry paper should be used each time.

Goldfish can live quite well in the conditions described so far, as long as they are not at all overcrowded and not overfed. But after a few weeks, you may find it necessary to add aeration and filtration to your aquarium. This can be added once the tank is well established or can be added when the tank is first set up. Actually, it's best to add aeration and filtration systems to the tank before it is stocked with goldfish. That way there will be fewer disturbances to the fish.

Aeration

The function of an aerator is to agitate the water, which exposes a greater amount of water surface to the atmosphere. This facilitates the absorption of oxygen from the air and the dissipation of carbon dioxide and other gaseous wastes from the water. An aerator is simply an apparatus that introduces a regular supply of air into the water via a stream of bubbles. That apparatus can be a small piston pump or a diaphragm vibrator which is simply called a vibrator pump. Both are available in various price ranges, but the piston pump, which is much more efficient than the vibrator, is much more expensive, too. A piston pump will produce enough air to operate a number of aquariums at one time. But for the beginner or the fancier with only a few tanks, a vibrator pump is usually more than adequate. There are some good vibrators available for only a few dollars.

The air pump pushes air into the tank through a small gauge plastic hose to which an airstone has been attached. Airstones are manufactured from a porous material through which the air is forced and emerges in water as continuous streams of tiny bubbles. The airstone can be hidden from view by placing it behind a rock. It must be secured or it may float to the surface of the water. This can be done by placing the rock over the airline connected to the airstone or by burying the airline under the gravel allowing only the airstone to protrude.

Filtration

To keep the aquarium crystal clear, a filter should be added. There are several types of filters available, but the simplest, the least expensive and in most cases the most practical for a small aquarium is the inside box filter, sometimes called an airlift filter. This filter consists of a small plastic box that is filled with a filtering medium such as polyester floss and/or carbon and a riser tube that protrudes up out of the top of the box. Air is introduced at the bottom of the riser tube inside the box either by another narrow diameter tube attached to the riser tube or by an airline that fits down the center of the riser tube. Some box filters even have an airstone at the bottom of the riser tube. Air bubbles flow up the riser tube thereby creating a water current that flows into the box, through the filtering medium and up the riser tube. Particulate matter such as fish droppings, food particles and mulm is drawn into the box and trapped in the filtering medium, while clean, particle-free water is emitted at the top of the riser tube. The higher the riser tube, the more efficiently the filter works, since clean water is carried further away from the dirty water entering the filter. A shorter riser tube allows a greater amount of clean water to be mixed with the water being drawn into the filter, so it will take longer to clean all of the water in the tank. Ideally, the riser tube should terminate just under the surface of the water. If the riser tube that comes with your filter box is not long enough to reach the water surface, a small piece of rigid plastic tubing can be purchased from your dealer and added to the riser tube. The filter will work without this addition, but will work much better with it. The filter can be concealed behind rocks or plants in the tank so that it does not become an eyesore in your aquarium. The use of the inside filter box usually makes it unnecessary to also have a separate airstone operating in the tank, since this device aerates and filters the water at the same time.

There are other types of aquarium filters available. One is the undergravel filter, which utilizes bacteria in the gravel bed as the filtering medium. It is a good system for a tank that is 10 gallons or larger in size, but is difficult to use properly in a small tank or bowl. It must be installed at the same time the tank is first set up.

Another type of filter used on a 10-gallon or larger tank is the motor-driven power filter. This is by far the best mechanical filter, but it is also the most expensive. In addition, it should not be used on a small tank, because it produces a water current that would be too strong for a small fish to handle in the confines of a small aquarium. In a larger tank the current would not be as strong.

(1) Power filters are very helpful in larger aquaria. They are available in sizes that pump as little as 100 gallons per hour (for 10-gallon aquaria), all the way up to king-size models capable of turning over nearly 1,200 gallons of water per hour. To set up a goldfish aquarium, the gravel should be thoroughly washed. This can be done right in the aquarium (2) or in a separate container. (3) Whichever way it is done, the gravel should not be used until the rinse water flows off clear. (4) Care must be exercised in planting rooted plants. They are at first pushed into the gravel rather deeply to make sure that all the roots get buried. Then the plants should be partially pulled out of the gravel so that the white crown area at the bottom of the leaves just shows. Photo by G. Timmerman.

43

(1) Emersed plants add a decorative touch to a garden pond. Photo by Laurence E. Perkins. (2) Koi are attractive fish for garden ponds because they are bred to have their color pattern on the back for viewing from above. Photo by Dr. Herbert R. Axelrod.

The

Garden

Pond

Many varieties of goldfish are at their best in outdoor ponds, and the advantages of keeping them in ponds are many—there are no aeration problems, as the large surface area allows a substantial interchange of gases to take place, plants will grow more freely and there will be plenty of beneficial natural foods available for the fish.

Methods of Pond Construction

There are many methods of constructing a garden pond, and it is not a project that should be rushed into without first giving it some serious thought. Three techniques will be considered here, each having its own special merits, but the choice must be left to the individual.

Primary consideration must be given to the location of the pond. It should not be built too closely to deciduous trees, because falling leaves in autumn can cause no end of trouble. Leaves must be continually removed from the pond or they will sink, decompose and upset the balance of a mature pond. The ideal site for a pond is one that receives sunlight on about half of its surface for most of the day. This ensures that the goldfish always have access to shade and that the water will not become too hot.

Molded Ponds

The first type of pond to be described is a commercially produced fiberglass or plastic-molded pond. These are rigid forms molded into a desirable shape. They are usually of an informal design; that is, they have varying depths and shapes. They are the simplest ponds to set up because all that is required is to excavate a hole the same size as the molding. Care should be given to remove any sharp stones lying in the hole, as the weight of the water in the pond mold could damage the mold and cause leakage. When the mold has been set firmly into the ground and dirt rammed into the empty space down the sides, the rim of the pond can be concealed with flat rocks. Plants can be planted around the edges and between the rocks to give the pond a more natural appearance.

Lined Ponds

The second type of pond is slightly more difficult to construct but is the least expensive. In fact, all you'll need to buy for it is a large piece of heavy gauge plastic sheet. First, dig out an area having the required shape and size. A minimum depth of two-and-one-half feet is recommended at the center of the pool, and the bottom should gently slope upward, reaching ground level at the edges. When the hole has been excavated, the area should be raked carefully to smooth out the contours and remove stones.

The polythene sheeting is then laid into the hole, shaping it to the bottom and having it bordering the edge of the pond. On this border are placed heavy rocks that will camouflage the sheeting and at the same time hold it in place. The excavated dirt can be piled around the rear and possibly on one or two sides of the pond to make a rock garden. As the pond is filled, the weight of the water will press the sheeting into the small contours of the bottom. Plants must be installed potted in this kind of pond so that their roots are not able to penetrate the plastic sheeting.

Concrete Ponds

The third and final type of pond to be described is the concrete pond. This is usually the most expensive and the most difficult to construct, but it is well worth the effort and money, because it is unquestionably the most permanent and reliable. With careful planning and a few weekends' work, the enthusiast can construct a landscaped pond that will provide an ideal home for his goldfish and will be an object of pleasure for many years.

Before beginning to plan the pond, it must be decided whether the pond is to be formal or informal in design. This decision will depend upon the existing layout of the garden. A plan of the pond should then be drawn and the siting, size, type of subsoil and drainage should be considered before construction begins. A formal pond is usually slightly easier to construct because its sides are straight and simpler to cast. The shape of the pond should be marked out on the site. This is done by using pegs and string. The thickness of the walls must be taken into account when the pond is marked out. The walls should slope slightly inward from the bottom toward the center of the pond so that when the pond freezes over, the ice will push upwards instead of pushing squarely against the walls of the pond.

A drain will be very helpful when it comes time to empty

the pond for cleaning. This should be situated at the deepest point in the pool and should allow the water to drain into your main underground drainpipe or into a soakaway which is a depression in the ground into which the water will flow and naturally drain away. A bathtub plug with the metal ring removed will be adequate as a stopper and it's a good idea to have a piece of plastic mesh positioned in the drain to prevent debris from clogging the pipe. The soakaway should be three times the volume of the pool and should be filled with large size gravel and stones. This will allow the entire contents of the pool to be drained at once. It is quite satisfactory to have a smaller soakaway and empty the bulk of the pond water first by siphoning it to a lower ground level. Then when the pool is almost empty, pull the plug and drain the remaining water into the soakaway.

An overflow pipe is very useful. It will retain a constant level in the pool and prevent it from flooding out during a heavy rain. A vertical plastic pipe connected to the drain can prove very satisfactory in maintaining the pond level. The pipe is simply screwed into a plastic socket that is fitted into the drainage hole and then cut to the height of the desired water level. Any water above the top of the pipe will run into the drainage system, thus maintaining a constant level in the pond. It's advisable to cover the end of the pipe with fine plastic mesh to prevent any floating debris or unsuspecting goldfish from being washed into the pipe.

After the hole has been excavated you can either line the hole with one hundred gauge polythene sheeting or pound about three inches of coarse gravel into the base.

Pouring the concrete is a two-step process but one which should be completed in the same day. Pouring the bottom and the sides on two different days or even too far apart in time on the same day could cause the pool to leak into the seams between the bottom and the sides. Pour the bottom first. Its thickness will vary with the size of the pond, but for a four-foot by six-foot pond that will be about two-feet deep, a four-inch-thick bottom is sufficient. After pouring about two inches of concrete into the bottom, wire mesh can be laid down to give the concrete greater strength. The remaining two inches of concrete are then poured over the wire. Make sure that none of the wire mesh protrudes out of the concrete. Before the bottom is poured, the side form should be made. It can be made from inexpensive exterior-grade plywood. It is essentially a pen whose shape is the same as the pool. If the pool is four feet by six feet, then the pen or form should be eight inches less in length and width. This will allow approximately a four-inch space around each side between the form and the earthen walls of the pool. The height of the form should be a few inches higher than the walls of the pool so that it can be easily removed after the concrete is set. Once the bottom is poured and smoothed, insert the form into the pool, spaced equally on all sides and allowing it to rest on top of the freshly poured bottom. Now the concrete for the walls can be poured between the earthen walls and the wooden form. Pour a few inches of concrete into each side in order to keep the form centered in the pool. Then each side can be filled up with concrete. Again, wire mesh can be inserted into the concrete to give it more strength.

An ideal concrete mixture is, by volume, one part cement, two parts sand and three parts gravel. The sand and cement should be mixed first, then add the gravel. Water should be added slowly until the desired consistency is reached.

Allow seventy-two hours for the concrete to set before removing the form. When the concrete has dried, paint the inside with watery cement. Do not allow this finishing coat to dry too quickly or it will not cure properly. Covering the suface with damp burlap will shade the pond from direct sunlight so that the finishing coat doesn't dry too quickly. If there is the likelihood of rain soon after the laying of the concrete, it is a good idea to cover the pool with polythene to prevent the rain from pockmarking the concrete surface. Once the cement finishing coat has dried, the pond should be filled with water and left alone for a week.

After the water in the pond has stood for about a week, the pond should be drained completely and the concrete surfaces scrubbed with a clean stiff brush. Now rinse the pond out thoroughly and allow it to dry. To make the pond completely leakproof, it is best at this stage to apply a coat of surface sealer. Several brands of sealer are manufactured especially for this purpose, all of which not only render the pond watertight, but also neutralize the effect of the lime in the cement which can be harmful to both the goldfish and the plants. The sealer should be applied following the manufacturer's instructions and allowed to dry. Then the pool should be filled once more with water, left for another forty-eight hours, drained, scrubbed and rinsed before preparation for stocking.

The landscape around the pond can now be constructed. A path of irregular paving or rocks can be laid around the edge of the pond, and the dirt excavated from the hole in which the pond was built can be used for the landscaping. With a little imagination, the whole area can be made to blend in with the total surroundings of the yard. It is a simple task to rig up a waterfall or fountain driven by a small electric pump. Such an addition not only increases the attractiveness of the pond but is also an asset to the health of the pond, providing good aeration which, as mentioned earlier, is not crucial, but is certainly helpful. Filtering devices can also be added to the pond.

Furnishing the Pond

In preparation for planting, two inches of clean coarse sand should be laid on the bottom of the pond. The best time for planting is spring because it gives the plants a chance to become well established before winter. There are many plants that are suitable for inclusion in a pond. Plants can be purchased from an aquatic nursery where instructions on planting and care are also obtained. No pond is really complete without a water lily or two. These are usually planted in submerged baskets near the center of the pond where they not only add a touch of beauty to the pond but also provide excellent hiding places for the fish.

After planting, the pond should be slowly filled with water. Placing a clean bucket on the bottom of the pond and trickling the water slowly into it will prevent the sand base from being stirred up.

Before introducing the fish into the pond it is best to wait at least two weeks to allow the water to mature. When the water has matured and the pond is ready for stocking, it is a good idea to introduce a few inexpensive goldfish at first in order to test the water. If they do well for a few weeks it is then okay to add some more expensive varieties. A few fresh water snails in the pond are beneficial, as they control the growth of excess foliage somewhat and also act as scavengers. If the pond is to be used for breeding, however, snails are best left out, as they will eat the fish eggs.

The maintenance of a well balanced pond should be a simple matter. Fallen leaves must be removed from the surface before they sink to the bottom of the pond, because their decomposition could foul the water. It may be necessary to empty and clean a small pond every year. The best time to do this is late autumn after the leaves have fallen. Plants should be thinned out, sludge removed, and the inside scraped clean of algae before refilling the pond with water. It is not necessary to change the sand and loam at the bottom of the pond unless the water has become polluted and the fish are dying. In that case the whole interior of the pond must be cleaned and disinfected with household bleach and thoroughly washed out so that no trace of the bleach remains. Larger ponds do not need to be cleaned out each and every year, but it wise to clean them at least once every other year. When the water has been completely changed, the fish should not be returned to it immediately, as the water must mature. During cleaning periods, the fish may be kept indoors in well aerated aquariums.

In the winter the surface of the pond may freeze over. The low temperatures will not harm most goldfish, but if the ice is left unbroken for long periods of time, a serious lack of oxygen can result. The ice should never be broken by tapping on it, because the resulting shock waves in the water could harm the fish. The best way to open a hole in the ice is to rest a hot kettle on it until the ice melts. If snow settles on the ice, it should be swept off in order to admit more light.

If your area is subject to severe winters, an extra precaution can be taken to prevent expanding ice from damaging the pond. Anchor a collapsible object such as a plastic bucket in such a way so that it floats on the surface. If the force of the ice becomes excessive, the bucket will be crushed, but the force against the walls of the pond will be eased, thus reducing the risk of cracks and leaks.

It will not be long after setting up a garden pond that various uninvited visitors appear. Many of these do no harm to the fish; in fact some, such as mosquito larvae, bloodworms and caddis fly larvae, are even beneficial, as they are scavengers as well as valuable food for the fish.

(1) While turtles such as this *Pseudemys* species and other local types appear to be good inhabitants for a garden pond, they really are not. They destroy plants, compete with the goldfish for food and may even eat the goldfish. Photo by Dr. P.C.H. Pritchard. (2) Bullfrogs, *Rana catesbeiana,* are highly predatory frogs and will eat goldfish greedily. They should be kept out of the pond. (3) Large water beetles can be very harmful to small goldfish. Photo by Laurence E. Perkins. (4) A water scorpion with open claspers. These are dangerous enemies of pond fishes. Photo by Laurence E. Perkins.

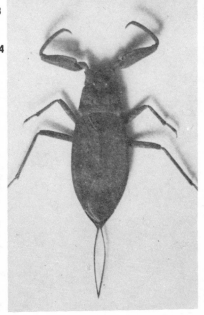

(1) A pair of veiltail goldfish in a spawning embrace. The eggs are laid over bushy vegetation. Photo by R. Zukal. (2) The pimple-like white spots on the opercula of this goldfish indicate that it is a ripe male that is ready to spawn. These spots are called breeding tubercles, and they slowly disappear once the breeding season is over. Photo by Laurence E. Perkins.

Breeding

Goldfish

After you've had the goldfish for a while, you might notice that some of them seem to be getting quite heavy. This might seem odd, since they are all eating about the same amount of food. It is likely that the heavier ones are females who are filling with roe (ripe eggs). This usually occurs in early spring, just prior to the beginning of the spring breeding season. A close look at the thinner goldfish may reveal tiny white "pimples" on the head and gill covers. These are "breeding tubercles" which appear only on males and only during the breeding season. Once the breeding season is over, the tubercles disappear.

There are two methods for breeding goldfish; one is the natural method in which the fish are bred in very large

aquariums or preferably in ponds, and the other method is by artificial insemination. Unless you intend to go into a large-scale breeding program, the pond method is preferred because it is simpler.

The Pond Method

One of the leading breeders of goldfish in the early part of the 20th century was Dr. Shinnosuke Matsubara. In 1908 he presented a paper in Washington, D.C. entitled "Goldfish and Their Culture in Japan." In this paper he described the entire breeding and rearing process of the well known "Ranchu" goldfish which is today known as the lionhead goldfish. Dr. Matsubara's method is as applicable today as it was in 1908 and serves equally well for nearly any of the goldfish varieties available. His method is described here.

When the breeding is carried out on a small scale, the usual number of parent fish is five, two females and three males. But for large-scale breeding it is best to use a 50-50 ratio of males to females. Spawning usually occurs anywhere from the beginning of April to about the middle of May. For the best results, careful attention should be given to the fish during September, October and November of the preceding year. During that time plenty of live food should be given to them, but without overfeeding them. The males should be separated from the females sometime before the breeding season begins.

As the spawning season approaches, the water in the pond should not be changed, but the goldfish should be amply fed with mosquito larvae, earthworms or tubifex worms for about ten days. At the end of the heavy feeding period, as the water temperature begins to rise or when it rains, spawning will occur. This usually happens when the water temperature has risen to about 60 to 65°F. A day or two before the anticipated start of the spawning, the water in the pond should be at least partially changed. The parent fish should be removed when the spawning is complete. The spawning bed consists of dense clusters of *Myriophyllum verticillatum* upon which the adhesive eggs are deposited usually the morning after the water change.

The pond size for five breeders should be three feet wide by four feet long and should be about five feet deep. Larger areas are required if more breeders are to be used. After the spawning is over and the breeders have been removed from the pond, the water in the pond should be drained quite low. Alternatively, the eggs can be removed by carefully lifting them out of the pond and placing them in shallow tanks containing water drained from the pond.

The eggs will hatch in eight to nine days when the water is kept at 60 to 65°F., and for a few days, while their last remaining yolk is being absorbed, the fry do not move about very much. For the most part they will stay on the gravel bottom or in the plant clusters. Three days after hatching the fry begin to swim free and feed. They can be fed at first with hardboiled egg yolk which has been strained through a piece of very fine cheesecloth. Mix the strained yolk with water until the water has a dense yellow color, then sprinkle the mixture over the entire tank. After seven days of feeding the fry with this egg yolk mixture they will be large enough to begin to feed on sifted *Daphnia* or *Cyclops* or on newly hatched brine shrimp. When the goldfish fry have fed on these small creatures for about 15 days they should be large enough to begin to feed on small mosquito larvae, finely chopped earthworms or tubifex worms.

Hand Methods of Breeding Goldfish

The entire secret for success in this method of breeding goldfish depends upon the proper selection of ripe breeding stock. The male must have a good supply of sperm and the female must be well loaded with ripe eggs. To test this criterion for the male, catch one in a net and press gently with one finger on his mid-section just above and slightly

1

2

3

This sequence of photos shows the courtship and spawning of a pair of veiltail goldfish. (1) The ripe male (as indicated by the breeding tubercles on its opercula) pursues and drives an egg-laden female. (2) The driving continues until the female (front) responds by stopping over the vegetation. (3) Gyrating side by side, both fish plunge down into the leafy plants. (4) Getting into the spawning position is sometimes cumbersome for the veiltail goldfish, because its short body shape has caused its swim bladder to be displaced. (5) Rolling over on their sides, the pair settles into the plants. (6) Eggs are finally expelled and fertilized. Photos by R. Zukal.

4

6

5

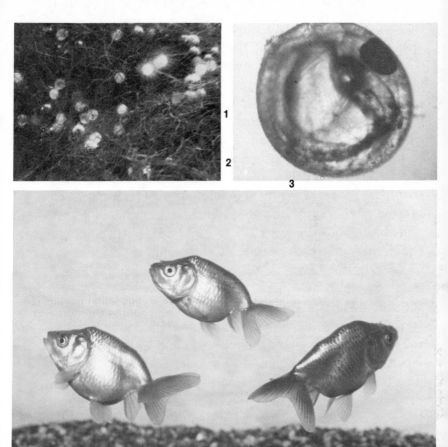

(1) Goldfish eggs. The clear eggs are fertile and the white ones are infertile. Fungus is growing on some of the infertile eggs. (2) A magnified view of a goldfish egg showing the developing embryo inside. (3) Three-month-old lionhead fry not yet showing any hood development. (4) Newly hatched goldfish fry clinging to the glass sides of an aquarium. Photos by Laurence E. Perkins.

forward of the vent. This should produce an excretion of a milky fluid from his vent; this fluid contains the sperm. The female is checked in the same manner except that you look for small yellowish eggs instead of white milky exudate. Once the pair has been selected, they should be placed into a small clean aquarium containing water from which they have been taken. The male should then be held in such a manner that his vent is below the surface of the water and the top part of his body above the water line. He should be squeezed gently as before but for a longer period of time as you move him about in the tank, spreading his milt throughout the water. Place him back in the pond or aquarium from which he came. The same thing should now be done to the female. If she is ripe enough, several thousand eggs can be produced. After all her eggs are "milked" she should be placed back in her original pond or aquarium. The water in the small tank should now be stirred for a minute or two so that the eggs and sperm will have a better chance of coming into contact with one another. The tank in which this artificial insemination takes place need not exceed one gallon in capacity, but could be a little larger if your breeders are fairly large. A clean mixing bowl can even be used for this purpose, but of course one fish cannot be kept in the bowl while the other is being milked.

About eight hours later the water should be poured out of the insemination tank. The eggs will be quite sticky and will adhere to the sides of the container. Pouring the water off rids it of dead and unfertilized eggs and the unused sperm. The small tank or bowl should now be placed into a much larger aquarium or pond containing only some old conditioned water from the original breeding pond and perhaps the beginning of an infusoria culture (microscopic organisms upon which the fry will be able to feed after they are free-swimming). The water in this aquarium or pond should be just deep enough to cover the insemination container by a few inches. When the eggs hatch and the fry show signs of moving about, they should be gently poured out of the small tank and into the larger quarters. From this point on the young are handled the same way they are in the natural breeding technique.

(1) Young water-bubble-eye goldfish at four weeks of age. Photo by Laurence E. Perkins. (2) A pair of celestials courting. Photo by Dr. Herbert R. Axelrod. (3) Young celestial just beginning to show protuberant eyes. (4) A five-month-old celestial. (5) A six-month-old celestial. Photos 3, 4, and 5 by Laurence E. Perkins.

(1) A frontal view of a good celestial specimen. Photo by G. Marcuse. (2) The head growth of an adult lionhead usually covers the cheeks as well as the top of the head. Photo by Laurence E. Perkins.

Goldfish

Varieties

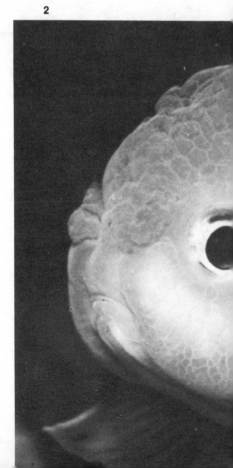

There are many different varieties of goldfish, and most of them are derived from the same original stock by the constant inbreeding of selected fish. Most of these varieties were originally developed in China and Japan. The original strains probably came from China, but the Japanese take credit for developing the more beautiful varieties.

All goldfish, regardless of their variety, have the same scientific name, *Carassius auratus,* but the only one that resembles its original ancestors very much is the common goldfish or "Wakin" (Japanese goldfish). This variety has a slender body and, when very young, its black pigmentation gives it the appearance of dull steel blue. The color gradually changes as the fish gets older to a vermilion red, often

with white patches. The tail is either forked or split into three or four lobes.

The famous "Ranchu" goldfish is also called "Maruko" (round fish) in Japan. In the U.S.A. it is called the lionhead goldfish. The body of this variety is short and rounded. The tail and broad head are also rather short. It has no dorsal fin at all. The head is free from any abnormal growths when the fish is very young, but as it matures it develops a mass of nodules on top of its head—the mass is usually fully developed by the time the fish is three years old. This mass has the appearance of the mane of a lion, thus the popular name, lionhead goldfish. Because of its globular body, short protuberant abdomen and very short tail, the lionhead cannot swim very smoothly. It normally swims with its head angled slightly downward. The lack of a dorsal fin is one possible reason for this abnormal swimming position.

The "Ryukin" or the Loochoo goldfish is more commonly known in the U.S.A. as the fantail goldfish. This variety has a short, rounded body with a swollen abdomen. The caudal fin, which is often much longer than in the fish's body, hangs limply when the fish is at rest but flows freely when it is in motion. All of the other fins of the fantail goldfish are also abnormally long and flowing.

A rare and exceptionally beautiful goldfish variety is the fantailed lionhead. In Japan this fish is known as the "oranda shishigashira" which means "rare lionheaded." This fish is about the same as the ranchu lionhead except that its body is bigger and longer than that of the ryukin (faintail) and it does have a dorsal fin.

The popular "telescope" goldfish is known in Japan as the "Demekin" (meaning goldfish with protruding eyes) or "Demeranchu" (lionhead ranchu with protruding eyes). This variety has protruding eyeballs and a short body and tail. The telescope-eye feature has been combined with the lionhead traits to produce a telescope lionhead goldfish that lacks a dorsal fin, has a globular body and the telltale lionhead feature. The eyes not only protrude out from the head but turn upward, too.

The famed Japanese "Shukin" goldfish (shukin literally means "autumn brocade") is a cross between the ranchu (lionhead) and the Loochoo (fantail). It is the same as the fantail lionhead (oranda) with the growth on its head and the long flowing fins, but is missing the dorsal fin. It is bred in many beautiful colors in Japan, hence the name "autumn brocade." It swims with great difficulty and must be kept separate from other goldfish varieties because it cannot compete for food with faster moving fish.

The most "common" fancy goldfish in the U.S.A. is one that still bears its original Japanese name, the "shubunkin." Literally translated, shubunkin means "vermilion red dappled with different hues." The shubunkin is a relatively plain goldfish as far as fin and body shape is concerned, and its only attractive feature is the variety of color patterns that have been bred into it. The shubunkin made its first appearance in Japan in 1900, where it was produced from ordinary goldfish stock.

More recent developments in goldfish breeding are the pearl-scaled fantail goldfish (China), the pompom goldfish (China) and the bubble-eyed goldfish (China). These are exceedingly rare, although more intensive breeding efforts should soon make them more readily available.

Other varieties appear whose scales seem to be colorless and give the fish the appearance of being scaleless. Actually, there are no scaleless goldfish. Such names as "scaleless" and "Calico" are common. Other names such as "Comet," "Chinese blue," "Midnight" and "Nymphs" are used to designate different fish in different places.

The young of most goldfish strains bear little resemblance to their parents. It usually takes from one to two years for young goldfish to develop their special characteristics. For this reason, mature fancy goldfish are quite costly, while young specimens are far less expensive.

(1) *Limnophila aquatica* forming emersed leaves. (2) With good strong sunlight, *Vallisneria gigantea* forms long tangles of leaves several feet high. Photo by T.J. Horeman. (3) *Sagittaria graminea* makes a good background plant in a goldfish aquarium. (4) *Vallisneria portugalensis* forms spiral leaves somewhat like those of the more familiar corkscrew val. (5) *Cabomba caroliniana* is a good spawning plant for goldfish. Photos 3, 4 and 5 by R. Zukal. (6) Water lilies are available in a variety of colors. Photo by Charles O. Masters.

4

5

6

(1) A variety of foods designed specifically to meet goldfish nutritional requirements are available. (2) Two well-nourished goldfish yearlings. The upper fish is a shubunkin male showing breeding tubercles on its opercula. The lower fish is a fine veiltail specimen. Photo by Laurence E. Perkins.

Foods

and

Feeding

One of the most frequent causes of premature death among goldfish is incorrect feeding. Overfeeding is one of the beginner's worst errors and is something that many people cannot resist doing. Fish eat far less than you might expect, and if they are given more than they can immediately devour, the food will sink to the bottom of the aquarium or pond and eventually pollute the water. As a general rule, never give the fish more than they can consume in five minutes. Also, try giving them foods which they can easily find and swallow. Avoid using both small and excessively large food particles.

The foods fishes prefer vary tremendously among dif-

1

(1) The bubbles on the water-bubble-eye goldfish are very delicate and rupture easily. Photo by Klaus Paysan. (2) Most of the emphasis in the lionhead or Ranchu is on the hood development and the shape of the body, a straight smooth back profile being most desirable. (3) Many goldfish varieties can be kept in a community pond or tank, except for the special breeds such as water-bubble-eyes and lionheads, which are not very competitive as far as feeding is concerned. (4) This oranda has a few nacreous scales and ragged fins. It is not a good specimen. (5) A comet with extreme fin development.

2

3

4

5

ferent species. Some fishes are carnivorous, and some are herbivorous, but the vast majority are omnivorous, which means that they consume both animal and vegetable matter. Goldfish are omnivorous and should be fed accordingly, using both animal and vegetable matter in the diet.

Many excellent brands of dried foods are available that contain a nearly complete balanced diet for fish. These foods are sold in various forms such as flakes, powders and compressed tablets. All are specially designed for various types of fishes and contain the correct proportions of carbohydrates, proteins, fats, vitamins and minerals required to keep the fishes in prime condition. "All purpose" foods may be supplemented with live foods such as tubifex worms, brine shrimp and ants' eggs. Goldfish have been known to live for years on a diet of dried fish food alone, but they cannot be compared as far as growth, finnage and color are concerned with fish whose diet has been supplemented with live food.

Many household foods may also be given as a supplement to the daily diet, although such commodities should not become the sole diet as they are often lacking in certain vitamins. Bread crumbs, breakfast cereals, boiled potatoes, shredded spinach or lettuce, minced lean beef and many other table foods can be offered to the fish in small quantities. These foods make a welcome change to the normal basic diet and are usually eaten greedily by most goldfish.

The value of live foods in the diet should not be underestimated. The results of their use make it well worth the extra trouble necessary to obtain various suitable invertebrates for this purpose. Some live foods such as tubifex and *Daphnia* are often available in tropical fish shops, and the small quantities required may be obtained quite cheaply. Tubifex are small reddish brown worms that live on decaying matter in the bottom of rivers and ponds. Before feeding them to the fish they should be left under slowly running water for a few minutes to purge them of any harmful material such as certain bacteria that could harm the fish.

Daphnia or "water fleas" are small free-swimming crustaceans that can be caught in almost any pond with a fine mesh net. Before they are fed to the fish, they should be examined and any other creatures caught with them should be removed. A water bucket or similar container placed in the garden can be an asset to the fish keeper by providing useful live food during the summer months. A few sprigs of elodea or other hardy water plants should be placed in the bucket to help keep the water pure and encourage the proliferation of various invertebrates. *Daphnia* may be kept in a water bucket or tub and will multiply freely; mosquito larvae will also appear. Mosquito larvae are not likely to harbor any parasites or diseases, but their disadvantage is that any surplus must be kept refrigerated to prevent them from metamorphosing into adult mosquitoes. Freshwater shrimp and other small crustaceans introduced into the tub will breed and provide a continuous supply of fresh live food.

Earthworms are one of the most valuable live foods and are especially useful during the breeding season. Whole earthworms are usually too big for small to medium size fish, but large pond-raised goldfish can consume them whole. For smaller fish, the worms must be chopped into smaller pieces. A good method for trapping earthworms is to place a quantity of leaf mold and natural manure into a hole dug in a shady part of the garden. One or two square yards will be ample space. Cover this with damp sacks which are kept moist on dry days by sprinkling them with water. The worms may be collected at weekly intervals by simply lifting the sacks. The worms will be found on the soil surface in large numbers. Early morning collection produces the greatest yield. Worms should not be collected more than once a week, however, or the supply will dwindle quickly.

(1) This goldfish pond was built above ground using large boulders and cement. Note the almost natural-looking waterfall. Photo by Laurence E. Perkins. (2) The statue and the brick edging give this pool more of a formal look. (3) This pool will be shaded by trees in the background for part of the day. (4) Informal goldfish pools. Photo by Paul Stetson.

(1) Emersed plants give a pool a natural look, provide shade and shelter for the goldfish and shelter for organisms that goldfish often feed upon. (2) A pool such as this gives a garden a very formal look. (3) The spraying fountain in this pool, in addition to having a decorative effect, has several practical functions, too. It aerates the water and helps to keep it cool on hot summer days.

Whiteworms are another valuable food, especially for smaller goldfish. Cultures of these can be purchased from fish shops and are quite easy to cultivate. To breed whiteworms, the following method is recommended. A shallow box approximately two inches deep (a plastic cat litter tray is excellent) is filled with a mixture of sifted earth and leaf mold. This is lightly dampened and the worms are scattered over the surface. A few pieces of stale white bread are placed around the soil surface as food for the worms. A sheet of glass is placed on top of the tray and the whole box is then covered with a folded sheet of newspaper to prevent light from entering. The culture should be left alone for about three weeks to allow the worms to multiply. The compost should be kept damp and the culture kept at room temperature, as the worms will not breed below about 50°F. They will collect on the underside of the glass cover, and it is then quite a simple task to scrape them off with a knife. If a few culture trays are used, it is possible to have an unending supply of this excellent food available. The idea is to start a new culture every three weeks. This means that each culture has a life span of six weeks and a new one will always be ready for use when an old one is discarded. Each new culture is started using a few worms from an old culture.

As mentioned previously, the correct feeding of fishes is very important, and when possible they should be fed at the same time every day, preferably once in the morning and once in the evening. The food should always be placed in the same spot in the aquarium or pond, and the fish will soon learn to anticipate feeding time—they will congregate at the surface when they detect activity. If for any reason a meal is missed this will cause no harm to the fish, provided that this does not happen too often. Most fish can live quite happily for up to three or four weeks without being fed, and during this time they will obtain some nourishment by nibbling at the water plants and the algae growing in the pond or aquarium. It is not, however, recommended that they be allowed to go without being fed for so long a period of time very often.

Because fishes are cold-blooded creatures, their rate of metabolism decreases at low temperatures and they therefore require less food. In fact, if the temperature is below 50°F. they will not feed at all. Smaller quantities of food should be given during the cold months, and in the outdoor pond they need not be fed at all in the winter. Foods containing high percentages of fats should be avoided in cooler weather because they are too difficult for the fish to digest at that time.

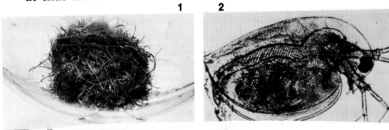

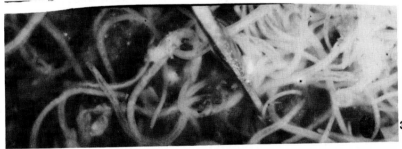

Live food organisms for goldfish. (1) Tubifex worms. Photo by Dr. Herbert R. Axelrod. (2) *Daphnia* is a good food for small goldfish. Photo by Knaack. (3) White worms can be cultivated easily in a box of dirt. Photo by E. Stansbury. (4) Ants and ant larvae are a nutritious goldfish food. Photo courtesy of American Museum of Natural History.

1

2

(1) A good red cap oranda. Note the well formed hood and the localization of the red pigment to the hood. (2) Veiltails are bred for the egg-shaped body and long finnage. Photo by Laurence E. Perkins. (3 and 4) Orandas were the ultimate result of a cross between a veiltail and a lionhead, or Ranchu. They have the hood of the lionhead but the dorsal fin and body shape of the veiltail. Photos by Kochetov.

3

4

(1) Predacious water beetle larvae are one of the principal enemies of goldfish kept in ponds. Photo by G. Timmerman. (2) A close-up view of "ich" on a goldfish. Each white nodule is an encysted parasite. Photo by Dr. G. Schubert.

Diseases,

Injuries and

Parasites

Goldfish are hardy and adaptable creatures. When they succumb to parasites, fungi or virus infections, it is usually because they have been weakened by a poor environment.

Symptoms to watch for in ailing goldfish are:

1. Loss of appetite
2. Sluggish and aimless swimming
3. Folded or clamped fins
4. Hanging from the surface or lying on the bottom
5. Slow reactions to disturbances
6. Rubbing against surfaces as if trying to scrape something off its body
7. Loss of luster
8. Ragged fins, lesions, spots or bumps

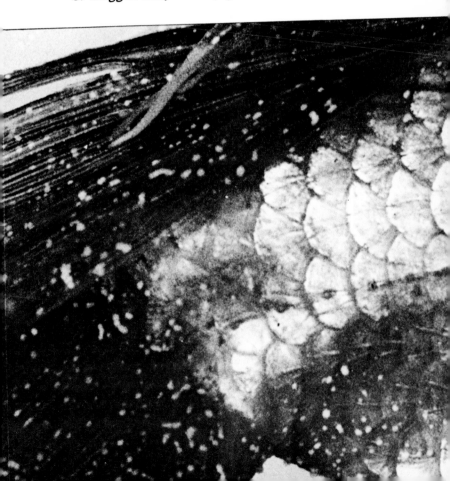

1

(1) Uniformity of the eye sacs is a desirable trait in bubble-eye and celestial bubble-eye goldfish. Photo by H. Hansen, Aquarium Berlin. (2) The celestial goldfish is very often seen swimming in this head-down position. Its lack of a dorsal fin and its anteriorly reduced and posteriorly enlarged swim bladder may be the cause of this odd swimming behavior. Photo by Kochetov. (3) These are unmodified *Carassius auratus.* It is from fish like these that most of today's fancy goldfish varieties are derived.

2   3

9. Bloating or emaciation
10. Gills that are pale rather than flushed with a healthy red color

Exotic goldfish are more vulnerable to diseases than the simpler varieties are and require more care. Fry are exceedingly delicate and are nearly impossible to successfully treat for diseases.

If your goldfish exhibit any of the above symptoms, consider carefully what might have caused the trouble:

1. Have there been any new fish or plants introduced into the aquarium or has water of doubtful purity been added, possibly introducing parasites or diseases?
2. Is there adequate aeration, are the fish over-crowded or has their environment generally deteriorated?
3. Have the fish been handled roughly or has the water been changed without the proper precautions on temperature adjustment or chlorine removal?
4. Have the fish been fed inferior or improper foods or has the water been polluted by adding more food than the fish can eat?

The above questions should be considered carefully as their answers might provide a clue as to what is wrong with your goldfish. Often troubles can be eliminated simply by correcting the problems in the environment, but sometimes chemical treatment is necessary.

Medications can be administered either by direct application to the affected area or by dissolving them in the water, depending upon what the medication is and what you are trying to cure. If the substance is to be dissolved, be sure that there are no undissolved particles remaining or these may be eaten by the fish, and this could bring about disastrous results. To make sure there are no undissolved particles of medication being introduced into the tank, filter the solution through a clean piece of linen or a brine shrimp net before adding it to the water.

Many patented drugs are available for treating specific diseases, and the average aquarist is usually well advised to stay with these. Be wary of any substance that is claimed to be a cure for everything.

If individual goldfish are showing any disease symptoms, they should be isolated immediately. If the entire pond or aquarium is affected, then large scale measures must be taken. If the exact trouble is not known, general first aid measures must be taken. A water temperature of at least 60°F. must be maintained, adequate aeration must be provided and only live food should be fed. The water level should be lowered to four to six inches so that distressed fish do not have to struggle to reach food and the well-oxygenated surface water.

The Hospital Tank

If individuals require treatment, they should be isolated from the rest of the goldfish to prevent possible spread of the malady with a resulting epidemic. A small hospital tank should be maintained for this purpose. It should contain no gravel or plants. It should have a stable temperature and should be situated in a quiet place away from bright lights where the fish will not be excited or disturbed. When the fish is transferred to the hospital tank, as much of its original water as possible should be included to minimize the shock of transfer.

The use of an isolation tank prevents a sick fish from infecting healthy fish. Medications can be used freely in it without worrying about killing plants and other beneficial organisms that normally inhabit tanks and ponds. More accurate dosages can be administered because of the smaller volume of water in the isolation tank. Healthy fish will not be able to harass weakened individuals, and once treatment is completed the tank can be easily sterilized.

An ailing fish can be noticed quickly in an aquarium, but in a pond, where there are many fish and many places for

(1 and 2) Telescope-eyed lionhead goldfish. The hood has not yet started to develop on these fish. Sometimes it doesn't develop at all, but usually it begins to show at about 18 months of age. (3) The smooth back profile of this celestial makes it a perfect specimen. Photo by H. Hansen, Aquarium Berlin. (4) Three varieties of the veiltail (l. to r.) metallic, matt and calico. (5) A most unusual veiltail is this blue-finned variety. Photo courtesy of the Copenhagen Aquarium. (6) An 18-month-old pearlscale undergoing a color change. (7) A three-year-old calico London shubunkin. Photos 1, 2, 4, 6 and 7 by Laurence E. Perkins.

5 6

7

them to hide, it is not so easy to detect the symptoms of a disease until quite a few fish have been affected. The pond keeper must therefore always be on the alert. If any fish appears to be slightly off color or behaves abnormally in any way, it should be netted out and placed in an isolation aquarium.

Disinfecting the Fish

A strong salt bath is the most effective method of disinfecting goldfish, particularly when they have open sores that leave them vulnerable to infection.

One pound of non-iodized salt should be dissolved in three gallons of water. For this it is best to use some of the water the fish are already in. The netted fish should be dipped into this solution for a minute or so, then immediately transferred to freshly aged water in the hospital tank. The fish may be stunned for a short time but will soon recover. Some of the mucous coating may be shed but this won't harm the fish if it is isolated for awhile.

Injuries

Injuries are usually due to rough handling but they can also be caused by vigorous spawning activities, other fish, birds or insects. Injuries that do not cause the immediate death of the fish will usually heal themselves, but the goldfish should still be protected against infection. The injured fish can be netted and the wounds dabbed with tincture of iodine. A small coating of petroleum jelly can then be smeared over the wounds and the fish should then be placed in isolation for awhile.

Surface Hanging

Surface hanging can be a symptom of overcrowding, pollution, or gill flukes. The pollution could be caused by decomposing organic matter or a high concentration of metal, particularly copper, dissolved in the water while passing through the water pipes. Never place copper or brass objects in an aquarium, and before using fresh water, it should be run for a minute or so to allow water that was in the copper pipes to run out.

Gas Bubble Disease

This problem is caused by excessive oxygen or other gases dissolved in the water, usually due to excessive plant growth together with strong sunlight. The problem is more prevalent in the winter since cold water retains more gases than warm water does. Air bubbles will be seen adhering to the bodies and fins of the goldfish, and they will often float at the surface on their sides. The fish are experiencing excessive gases in their blood stream. This condition is similar to the "bends" experienced by deep sea divers. Long-finned goldfish seem more prone to suffer from gas bubble disease than short-finned goldfish. This problem can be easily remedied by placing the fish into fresh water that is free of any algae or by gently agitating the water to release the gases.

White Spot *(Ichthyophthirius multifiliis)*

These small spherical parasites appear commonly on tropical fishes and they can attack goldfish, too. The affliction is easily identified by the minute white spots initially scattered over the body and later covering the head and gills. Once the gills have become affected, respiration will be impaired and the fish may soon suffocate. Fish frequently rub themselves against objects in the aquarium in an attempt to ease the irritation.

There are patented medicines made largely of malachite green that are available for this condition, but an experienced aquarist may be able to treat an affected fish by placing it in a hospital tank and gradually increasing the temperature to just over 85°F.

In a pond where the problem is persistent, disinfection

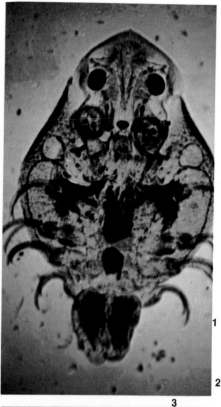

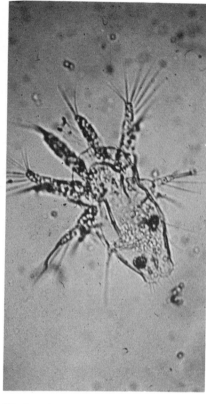

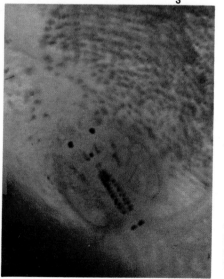

(1) *Argulus* often attack goldfish kept in ponds. Photo by Dr. E. Elkan. (2) A larval parasitic copepod, *Lernaea cyprinacea.* Photo by F. Meyer. (3) Fish lice attached to a carp. Photo by Dr. Pierre de Kinkelin. (4) An adult *Lernaea cyprinacea,* a parasitic copepod. Photo by F. Meyer. (5) *Lernaea cyprinacea* attached to the skin of a goldfish. These parasites are sometimes known as anchor worms. Photo by Frickhinger. (6) A highly magnified view of free-swimming ich parasites. Photo by Dr. Reichenbach-Klinke. (7) Ex-ophthalmus (pop-eye) and scale protrusion (dropsy) are usually caused by an internal bacterial infection. Photo by Frickhinger.

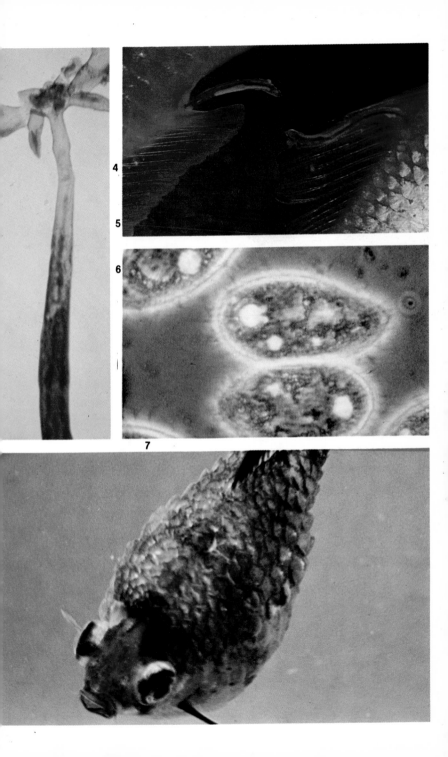

4

5

6

7

may be necessary. The fish should be removed from the pond and chlorinated lime should be introduced into the water. After a day or two, the disinfectant can be neutralized by adding the same quantity of sodium thiosulphate to the water. The pond should then be drained, rinsed and refilled.

Anchor worm

Anchor worms are small free-swimming parasites that get their name from the shape of the head. They burrow into the flesh of the fish leaving only the egg sac protruding. It is the egg sac that reveals the presence of the parasite. It is often up to one-half-inch in length and can be easily seen. These parasites are often seen behind the dorsal and pectoral fins. Soon afer one attaches itself, a red blood spot will be seen at the point of entry. When the fish is lifted out of the water, the worm contracts into a small fleshy blob.

Using a cotton swab, the individual parasites should be painted with either turpentine or kerosene. This softens the parasite and enables it to be easily removed with tweezers, thus causing the minimum amount of damage to the fish. If an attempt is made to remove the parasites without first killing them, pieces of fish flesh will be pulled out with the parasites. Particular care must always be taken when removing them near the eyes or gill membranes. Once they have been removed, the affected areas should be painted with an antiseptic such as Mercurochrome to guard against bacterial infection.

Fish Louse

This free-swimming parasite is very difficult to detect because it is fairly translucent and fastens itself tightly against the body of the fish. It is flat, round, approximately one-eighth of an inch in diameter and possesses a small proboscis between its eyes which it uses to extract blood from its host. It is often found on the belly, gills and throat of a fish. It can live up to three days without a host and lays rows of eggs on the aquarium glass.

A good indication that fish lice are present in the tank or pond is when the goldfish rub themselves against objects in an attempt to scrape the parasites from their bodies. Often they cause more damage to themselves in this manner than the fish lice cause. In a severe attack, the fish can become so weak that they die. Affected areas become inflamed and flushed in color.

For the aquarist working on a small scale it is usually simplest to remove the parasites individually by painting them with either turpentine or kerosene and then removing the dead parasites with tweezers.

If a severe attack has become established, it is best to make a solution of one gram of potassium permanganate to 22 gallons of water. Then immerse the fish for approximately 20 minutes every ten days until all of the parasites have been exterminated. This repetition is necessary because the parasites in the egg stage are not affected.

Flukes

These parasites are barely visible to the naked eye, and they can only be suspected until the infestation is severe. Affected fish swim in an erratic and jerky manner and usually appear to be exhausted. The fish may twitch and attempt to scrape the flukes off by rubbing their bodies against objects. The growth of the fish will be retarded and, in severe cases, the flukes may be visible underneath the gill covers. Blood may also be visible on the skin.

Flukes are free-swimming parasites that flourish best in an overcrowded tank. They are usually lethal to fry. If flukes are suspected in any fish, all of the fish in the same environment must be treated for the parasite.

A solution of 2 ml. of 40% formalin for every 2.25 gallons of water will kill the flukes. Immerse the fish for approximately 30 minutes or until it appears to be in distress.